Jack Francis

Pawnshops and Lard

V·O·L·C·A·N·O
PUBLISHING

Volcano Publishing,
13 Little Lunnon,
Dunton Bassett,
Leics. LE17 5JR

First published 1989

Second edition 1990

Printed and bound in England by
Bassett Enterprises Ltd.,
Leicestershire.

Phototypeset in 12pt Baskerville.

ISBN 1 870127 26 9

Acknowledgements

To Birmingham Public Libraries
for kind permission
to reproduce photographs on
pages 6, 20, 22, 28, 32, 40, 59, 64, 76, 78, 79, 80 and 81

The two letters on page 55
and illustrations on pages 4, 53 and 60
reproduced by kind permission of the
'Birmingham Post & Mail'.

To various members of my family
without whose encouragement
this book would not have been produced.

*Dedicated to the memory
of my long suffering mother.*

Preface to the Second Edition

The reaction of readers to the first edition was generally that they thought the trials and tribulations of those times were something that had only happened to them. It was a relief to read that they were not alone in suffering from bugs in the bedrooms and the continual journey to and from the local pawnshop.

However, many asked if there was a possibility of Jack Francis having any more of his fascinating stories – nay facts – of life in those times and be able to produce a second edition.

So as not to alter the original format of a Diary and Reflections in the first edition, the additional material has been added as Part III – *Further Reflections*.

There are some additional interesting photographs of the period as well, for some of which we are again indebted to Birmingham Public Libraries.

November 1990

Contents

List of Illustrations

A typical back to back house of the period.

Introduction – 'Hearth and Home'

To try and make the reflections more interesting to the reader, I have written in the style of a diary kept by a young lad during the formative years of eight and fourteen.

I was born in 1920, in a back street of the Nechells, a district of Birmingham into a family already containing two brothers and five sisters, aged from a few months to nineteen. We lived in a three roomed house consisting of a living room, bedroom and attic. Eight of us children, including the teenagers, slept in two beds in the attic. The bedclothes were one sheet and a pile of bug infested old coats.

The toilets were at the top of the yard or terrace, and there always was – being so many of us – a bucket full of urine in the middle of the attic floor. On top of the contents were always a couple of dozen bugs floating that we had plucked from the beds before getting in, knowing that there would be a great deal more when we woke up next morning. The hundreds of fleas were harder to catch.

We had no electricity, gas, or even water in the house and the attic was lit by just one candle – but more about that later. However, this did not mean that my mother, brothers and sisters were dirty. On the contrary, they were scrupulously clean and would scrub the bare boards of the attic and bedroom together with the quarry tiled floor of the living room. In fact the bare wooden table in the living room was as white as snow through continual scrubbing. You could see your face in the polished cast iron fireplace. It seemed that even the best of people living in the back streets had bugs and fleas. Large families of children were common in those days as was the problem of bed-wetting.

Even though my father was always unemployed, he always managed to get his beer, and even though he was not cruel to us kids, we used to dread his drunken footsteps coming up the path. This was because, at night, my mother would say 'Get to bed quick, ya dads a-coming'. We dreaded it because we knew there would be a fight or a row, in fact one of my sisters told me that for many years after she had married, and years after my father had died, she still woke at night to the sound of the old man's drunken footsteps.

My mother washed and pawned for years and years from Monday to Friday. Everybody's and anybody's washing and then stand for hours ironing it all. In between, she would go out and scrub floors, and all for a few bob (*old shillings*). There's many a bundle, of other people's clothes, gone into the pawnshop to feed our hungry mouths. But there were some good souls about in those days and I'm sure they knew my mother was pawning their washing but didn't say anything as long as the washing was done and ironed for the weekend.

I know for a fact that one of two neighbours had lent my mother some bits of washing that she had washed and ironed for them, (without any payment). This allowed her to pawn them till the weekend so she had enough money to buy an evening meal.

The reader is sure to think "where did she get the money from to get all these clothes and washing out of the pawnshop each weekend?" That will be forever a mystery – if there was ever a case of robbing Peter to pay Paul this must be it – bearing in mind that the bundles were only pawned for as little as one or two shillings at the most. I admit my father did have his paltry unemployment pay, but if there ever was a medal for a mother striving to feed the mouths of her many hungry children, then I am sure she would have been awarded the equivalent of the Victoria Cross. More of this later in the diary.

Even though my two elder sisters and brother were working, they were only teenagers and my father being unemployed, the amount of money they put into the house would not have covered the lowest of a man's wage, and there were eleven of us to feed and clothe, with one more baby yet to come. My sisters could not get married quick enough, but they were good, proud, girls and they must have cried at having to leave my mother in such a poverty stricken state. My two older sisters married, another sister went into domestic service and my older brother left home. This left five children at home with another due any time.

Now a word about my elder brother, who at the age

Tram officials waiting in the mist outside the Junction Inn, Great Francis Street.

of sixteen, in 1926 left home and emigrated to New Zealand to work on a farm under a Salvation Army scheme. I would think that he left home partly for decency sake when you know that eight of the nine children at that time all slept in the attic, and five of them were girls aged eight to twenty and then there was myself plus two brothers. I cannot remember how we all slept in the two beds, but I should think that my older and younger brother plus myself in one bed and the five girls in the other bed. I mention all this because about three years after my brother had emigrated to New Zealand, he sent my mother £20 that he had saved. That was more than eight weeks wages for an adult manual worker at the time, you can imagine the jubilation in our household, I think we were the talk of the street for many a day.

Amongst many things our happy mother did, was to rig us all out in fine new clothes, then she had all the house decorated (wallpapered) which came to 7/6d for the living room, the same for the bedroom, ten bob for the staircase, five shillings to whitewash the attic – a grand total £1 10s to decorate four rooms – what would that cost to-day? I only wore my new suit for Sunday best, and it may be hard to believe that only a few weeks after my mother received the £20, my first ever new suit vanished, as did my younger sisters' dresses. I cannot recall crying when I realised that my lovely suit had been pawned, never to be seen again. On looking back, we younger children took this for granted as that was the way of things but I think I was allowed to keep my new boots. The £20 did not

Holte Armshouses, Aston Lane, Aston, c. 1926

last long and I know for a fact that my mother had lent or given a few shillings out of the £20 to two or three poor neighbours. We found ourselves back in the same position we were in before, with nothing now pawnable and with no food in the house. It is an uncanny thing, but I still have a photograph taken during that brief rich period of the £20 fortune. The photograph taken over sixty years ago shows, five of us younger children wearing our new clothes. Sadly we soon reverted back to our old selves with me in both ragged trousers and pullover. Sentimental though the photograph is, it somehow seems to rub salt into a happy dream, that never really happened.

My father had to eventualy go on what they called The Parish, which meant one foot inside the workhouse for all of us, but more about The Parish later.

I hope the reader will see some humour in the diary as well as the drama.

THE DIARY AND REFLECTIONS

January 1928

Have been at school nearly three years, it is a bitterly cold to day, 10.15 a.m. As usual, we were sent out to the school playground to eat our mid-morning lunch – our breakfast! My mother had put in for me the usual piece of toast wrapped in newspaper, it tasted like cold cardboard.

Reflections

A piece of cold toast or bread spread with margarine or lard was to be my mid-morning lunch for practically the whole of my nine years at school. All I wore was a cotton shirt and ragged pullover and trousers – coats and underwear were unknown to me. I was always blue with the cold. Most of the kids were like me, from poor families but one or two of the better-off kids would have an apple or orange or even a piece of cake. Over the course of time I had learnt the art of sucking-up to these kids to get the apple core before it was completely finished or thrown away, or better still a bite of cake. Some mothers who lived facing the school took hot toast and hot tea across to their children and passed it through the palings. I have stood looking and wishing many times that it was me being given the hot food and drink to warm me through. The better-off kids were few and far between in those days, but they were always wrapped up warm. I had a school mate who only lived a few doors away and his father had a good job. They had to my mind a nice home and even had a gramophone which to me was fantastic. The school mate was an only child at that time and I used to go in his house on a winters' evening to play with him. At about nine o'clock his mother would cook a bit of supper and during that time I would have one eye on my friend and one eye on the supper. I used to hope and pray she would not send me home without at least giving me a piece of bread dipped in the fat. I remember once she gave me a hot boiled potato on a piece of bread, and then sent me home. Can you imagine dawdling down a dark street on a winter's night munching hot potato and dry bread, you are eight or nine years old and always hungry, its wonderful.

February 1928
Its' my birthday today – I am eight. My mother gave me a penny, and I dare say I shall get a penny off my sisters and dad.

Reflections
Birthday cards and Christmas cards were practically unheard of amongst the poor families in those days, and I can't recall ever receiving a birthday present as such, although I would think my sisters would have brought me a bit of something at odd times, even though I was a holy terror and a dirty little scruff.

April 1928
Scalded my foot today, in terrific pain.

Reflections.
All of us kids were sitting around the fire and on the hob was a saucepan full of boiling water, I caught the handle and the boiling water went over my foot. I would not go to the

hospital but after a few days I had to as the flesh was in a bad way. That pain is still imprinted in my mind even today.

Xmas Eve 1929

Its' about eight p.m. on Christmas Eve and all of us kids are sitting with our hands in our laps, not saying a word and looking as though butter wouldn't melt in our mouths. The truth is, we can't get to bed quick enough to hang our stockings up hoping that Father Christmas would come. One of us makes a move to get undressed and my mother says "It's no good hanging your stockings up, there ain't nothing". We laid awake for what seemed hours and hours, hoping that she did not mean what she said.

I was the first to wake on Christmas Day and when I saw my bulging stocking I shouted "he's been, he's been". It's just like sounding the bugle of a cavalry charge and all us younger ones have gone berserk. I, for one, got an apple or an orange and some nuts, a bar of chocolate. a new penny and a small tin penny motor car. It's going to be a fantastic Christmas Day.

Reflections

Most Christmases were the same, not only for us but for all the poor kids, and when our mother said "there ain't nothing" little did we know how near the truth this was for many Christmases.

When all the kids at school and in the street are talking about hanging their stockings up and your mother tells you there is nothing, this with other setbacks, must leave a deep rooted effect for years to come.

June 1930

Woke this morning, Saturday, at about ten o'clock, I look through the attic window, the sun is shining and it looks like being a beautiful day.

As I make my way past the urine bucket with the bugs on the top, I can hear the gangs of kids shouting in the street – I can't get there quick enough.

Reflections

Perhaps we should now pause for a while and let me explain, especially for the younger readers and social history students, something of the times, atmosphere and some of the characters who lived in our street at that time.

There is one thing for certain, even though poverty can happen any time, when you think that in the early 1920s, most houses and families did not have electricity, gas, water, inside toilets, television, radio, record players, child allowance, social security, etc., etc., those days will never be seen again. In fact I am going to be so bold to say, that for most, this was the extreme tail end of the poverty that Charles Dickens wrote about.

This is an earlier picture than 1920, but there were hundreds of backyards like
this still in the '20s and only a short distance from the city centre.
Was it surprising that disease was common amongst children?

The Street

Can you imagine a long street at about mid-day on a hot summer Saturday, in the 1920s. The streets alive with people and screaming kids. There are dozens of horses and carts of all shapes and sizes, there's hawkers shouting out their wares, there's ex-wounded soldiers and unemployed men, singing or playing trumpets or banjo's begging for a copper or two. There's women fetching the old man's suit or bundle out of the pawnshop, the public houses are like beehives, with singing towards closing time.

The younger readers must bear in mind that the men were still sodden with four years of blood and mud from the battlefields of France, during the 1914-18 war, even though it is now several years later.

There's the Salvation Army band on the street corner, trying to convert us all. There's mothers going berserk with their shopping bags because they have been paid their weekend housekeeping money. There are dogs of all shapes and sizes barking. All in all to us kids Saturday, in particular, was one big happy variety show.

But to continue, this then was the street I was born and brought up in, full of back-to-back houses, nooks and crannies, and terraces, with pubs and a pawnshop within yards of each other. The kids and adults used to find their pleasure in the streets – 'though from the amount of kids, the adults found their pleasure in bed as well!

On a Summer's day and late in the evening, people would sit on their front doorsteps all down the street and call across to each other. The few that had a gramophone seemed to have the same record and only one record and in between the shouting of the kids you could hear the screeching music of *In a Monastery Garden* on one side of the record and *In a Persian Market* on the other side.

People were different in those days, everybody was in the same boat and so close to each other. You could be away from your house all day and never even think of locking the door. A young woman could walk anywhere in the middle of the night and would be as safe as safe could be.

But to continue with the street. There was the old fellow who used to play a banjo and sing outside the pub doors for a few coppers (pennies) wearing an old black frock-coat with tails, and a cloth cap, he always sang the same old song "She's my lady love". And there was an ex-naval man who used to have a gramophone in a pram, with his dog sitting by the side. There were groups of one-legged or one-armed ex-soldiers, singing or playing battered musical instruments, again for a few coppers. There were the salt sellers who used to come round with a hand-barrow and a saw and sell blocks of salt for a penny. There was also the man repairing wooden wash tubs, and who would shout, "Tubs to mend". There were men selling celery, peri-winks (winkles), pikelets, kippers and even crockery.

There used to be a man who came with a small fair roundabout (merry-go-round) on a horse drawn cart. The roundabout would hold about a dozen kids and the bloke had to push it around with his hands. The charge for this was not money but one empty glass jam-jar. He then would sell the jars to a glass factory for re-cycling. There was the knife grinder and his donkey and cart, and to top it all there amongst it all would be the barrel organ playing "Pack up your troubles in yer old kitbag".

One old fellow used to come round the houses offering to re-paint (in white) the house numbers for a penny (1d) and some folk agreed for pity's sake. Now our street was very long with a number of pubs. At that time beer was 4 pence (4d) a pint and ale was 6 pence (6d). I don't think the old fellow and his little brush and a small tin of white paint ever reached the other end of the street sober!

Another old character used to make mats out of old strips of rags and old coats. After every mat he made and sold, he used to go and get drunk – then it was back to the mats.

I would like to recap here with the reader to emphasise a point and to give a fuller picture before I continue. Having 8, 10, 12, or even more children in a family was a common thing in those days, so can you imagine what seemed like a couple of hundred kids galloping about in our long street. The streets were our television, and apart from that, good or bad, the likes of that great multitude of kids will never be seen again.

Here are some of the games boys like myself played.

Coppers on the cut.......Hopping Jenny.

Release......Marbles...

Kick the can......Jack Stones.

Weak horses......Rounders.

Cannon......Cigarette cards.

Tip cat......Tops, Knock down, Skimmers, and others.

The most uncanny thing about these games was that most of them had their own season without saying a word. There was a set time for Tip Cat and when one started to play Tip Cat, within a couple of days the whole district would be playing Tip Cat. One of the many things we boys used to do after school on a hot summer's day, was to go to the canal in Tyburn Road, Salford Bridge, for a swim. This was called the Sandbanks because there were clay and sand banks about ten feet high running down from the road to the canal. There would be crowds of kids absolutely stark naked behind the sandbanks swimming in the canal. Coming straight from school and on the spur of the moment we wouldn't have had swimming trunks and towels so we would just dry ourselves on our shirts. I have swallowed many a mouthful of that stagnant canal water and it wasn't unusual for a dead cat or dog to come floating past. All of a sudden there would be a shout "Coppers" and grabbing our clothes, such as they were, there would be naked bodies dashing in all directions, like hundreds of baboons on the run.

Now back to the street.

There was a newspaper seller who always needed a shave, he was alway running, and chasing the girls. He used to sell a mid-morning sports paper called the BUFF, and being a bit of a comic, we were all sure he used to shout Bum instead of Buff.

There was the celery man, who instead of shouting "Big hearted celery" which was the phrase in those days, he shouted "Kind hearted celery".

A lot of the old names have been forgotten, the water drains outside were called Suffs, the dustbins were called Miskins, a door was called Doer, a street or road was called Horse Roads, the wash-house in the middle of the yard was called Brewus,

A lot of the old cures for illnesses have gone, But in those days if you had chest trouble or whooping cough, you would be put to bed with a lump of tar put in a bag tied around your neck, or your chest rubbed with goose fat, or your mother would take you down to the gas works for an hour or so to inhale the gas fumes. If you had earache or wax in the ear, your mother would boil an onion and put the middle part, while still warm, in the ear. A boil would call for a hot bread poultice. If you had a sore eye, you would bathe the eye in warm tea leaf water and then put the tea leaves rolled in a bag on the eye again as a poultice. I bruised my foot once as a child and my mother said "watch it doesn't turn into a pigs foot". This worried me and for the next few days I would inspect the foot to see if it was still the same shape.

Most of the men wore big cloth caps in those days, and some of them were still working in bowler hats, even common labourers. Some of the lads wore caps when they first started work, but there seemed to be more cap then face. A lot of the women including my mother, wore the old men's caps, not to be in fashion like today, they had nothing else to wear. I have seen women who have been lucky enough to have a new coat, still wearing the old man's cap.

One of the things we kids liked to see was a gang of men digging holes in the street, There weren't any mechanical drills in those days only heavy long handled sledge hammers and a big steel spike. Four or five men would form a circle around the spike and like clockwork, each man would hit the spike with the hammer, this would go on until the concrete broke. We all stood around, open mouthed and with 'little devils horns', hoping one of the men would miss the spike, but they never did.

There were not many cars or vans about in the 1920s, at least not in the side-streets. In fact they were still delivering bags of flour by steam traction engine to bakeries nearby. All sorts of carts were horse drawn and there would be dozens of railway horses. It was a common thing to see a team of three or four big railway horses come passing by, dragging a big heavy load. The cracking of the whips and the shouts of the waggoner seemed to mingle with the hum and buzz that fitted the times. Most of the side streets were still cobblestones, and the cart wheels were steel bound, so

It was common to see teams of four or five horses but this is unusual with no less than ten horses. Imagine that coming along a city street today!

A horse drawn hearse, of the 1920s, for a child complete with rear coach for its parents to ride in.

you can imagine the noise.

There were the tall, jet black, beautifully groomed funeral horses with their shining harnesses. When a funeral came into sight, everybody would stop and stand still until the funeral had passed and the men would take off their caps. If the coffin had a Union Jack flag draped over it, this showed that the deceased was an ex-soldier or ex-sailor for men were still dying of war wounds from the first World War – men would stand to attention and salute.

There was a strange thing that went on in those days that seemed to have been handed down from one generation of children to another. With no disrespect to the deceased, but when a funeral passed, most of the children used to spit on the ground. This was a silly habit that should never have been, but as stupid as it was, it is uncanny to think that it could have been handed down from the time of the black plague. In fact a rhyme used to be recited by the children which went something like this:

Catch yer collar, never swaller in case yer catch a fever.
Not for yer, not for me and not for any of me family.
(then the children would spit on the pavement)!

The older people of the 1920s were of a different breed and it seemed that us children were seeing the door close on an era that had lasted from early Victorian times. During which time, even my own mother had left school at eleven years of age to start in domestic service.

This farm was only a few hundred yards from Alum Rock Road and a short distance from Saltley and Nechells.

22

When you think that houses had been lit with candles and oil lamps for hundreds of years. Yet houses were still being lit with candles and oil lamps, even in the centre of Birmingham in the 1920s. Meat was still being cooked on a hook in front of a fire, then surely the 1920s were the last link with history of a bygone age. That is why I think that people passing on the oddities and mannerisms of those times, have witnessed the last page in a very large chunk of Victorian history.

Back to the street and fairs.

You don't see the fairs in Brumigam of fifty years ago. I know there are fairs today, but in those days they were a way of life and were the highlight of the year. Whole families used to go to Pat Collins' Goose and Onion fairs, and this was the most exciting time of the year for us kids. Even though this has been written about before, but for the younger readers interest, there was the time when a lion escaped from the fair and caused some excitement amongst the kids, although I have forgotton the year.

They even used to drive cows down our street on the way to the market – there were still farms only a short distance away. Now and again a stray cow would go up an entry or terrace, to the alarm of the women and great excitement of us kids, and one cow even went into the pawnshop, that made us laugh I can tell you.

Although this photo' was taken before 1920, it shows a typical back street forge even in the 1930s.

24

There were the knockers up who used to go around knocking on people's bedroom windows with a long bamboo stick to get them up for work in the early hours of the morning. But this was already dying out for the alarm-clock had arrived, for those that could afford one. There were also the lamplighters who used to go around lighting the street lamps with a long pole.

There was May Day, when all the horses would be dressed up in flowers and ribbons in all the colours of the rainbow. There would be the horses of the City Corporation and different trades like the railway, milk, bread, coal, rubbish, rag, bottle or bone, knife-grinders donkey, hawkers donkeys and many others, all in trimmings and flowers. It was a sight worth seeing in those grim back streets at the time, and it gave a bit of magical pleasure to the kids who would be told "There aint nothing for yer stocking" on Christmas Eve.

There were the tripe, chitterlings and pigs feet shops, there were the rag and bone shops, and there was old Mr. Hunt, who could have stepped out of one of Charles Dickens' books, but more of those later. There was the man who used to play the spoon clappers all over his body, to the music of the barrel organ – that was a work of art. There was another character and his wife, the wife would play the barrel organ while he performed his antics. He was a real comedian, and he would make all of us kids sit on the edge of the pavement on both sides of the road, while

When we were kids and on some of the carts, we would run under the back and have a ride on the axle. We would also run under a horse's belly for a dare!

26

he performed his antics. He was a real comedian, and would make all of us kids sit on the edge of the pavement on both sides of the road, while he performed down the middle of the road. Sometimes he would dress up as a clown or Charlie Chaplin, complete with bowler hat, black tailed coat, baggy trousers, black moustache and cane,, As he danced and performed up and down the street, all to music and with the screaming kids, you would have sworn that it was Charlie Chaplin himself. I have seen horse and carts stop at both ends of the street while he performed, and indeed the drivers enjoyed the performance as well. In between the somersaults and spoon playing, the highlight would come when our comedian, still dressed up in his Charlie Chaplin clothes, would run across to one of the many mothers watching, get on one knee, hold her hand and sing to her to the music of the barrel organ, much to the screams of laughter of the other women and the kids. Even his poorly dressed wife on the barrel organ used to laugh, though she must have seen the act many times before.

Can you see the picture of all those ragged kids, sitting along the kerbs, not only from our street but from streets all around? The air would be full of laughing, yet spellbound, kids, the barrel organ, the spoon clappers, the singing, the clown, all from a dingy, dirty, back street of Brumagem in the 1920s, I shall never forget it. Another character was an old lady who came around the streets on a Sunday morning singing, "Count your blessings". They say she died worth hundreds of pounds.

To complete the picture of those times, perhaps one should mention the smell of sweating horses, hops from the many pubs, and the horse manure that was all over the streets.

This was Gosta Green, in 1934, where a rag market was held. The island and trees were not there in the 1920s.

The Diary – Part II

August 1930

All us kids in the family have caught the disease impetigo.

Reflections

One of the children caught impetigo, and within a few days the rest of the kids in the family had it. This consisted of festering sores over the body, and the reason why I have mentioned this is because of the woman at the school clinic, which was at Sheep Street in Gosta Green. My younger brother and myself had to go to the clinic everyday for about two weeks for a hot bath, and this woman, she must have been at least sixteen stone, well she used to drag me and my brother around the bath like two wet rag dolls, and she would go over us as quick as lightning, with a big piece of rough flannel and fetch all the tops off the sores. It is a little episode I shan't forget, and I dare say that one or two will remember the Sheep Street clinic, especially the girls and boys with nits.

September 1930

Went for the usual half a loaf, and two ounces of lard.

Reflections.

I would think that all the time I was at school, it was a ritual everyday after school for me to go across to the small shop for the top half of a cottage loaf and two ounces of lard. My mother would need more bread before the shop would shut, but the bread and lard would be a filler for us kids, until (in most cases) she had been to the pawn shop to get a couple of

Solid rubber tyres still used, late 1920s

30

bob for an evening meal, such as it was. The full cottage loaf cost 3$^1/_2$d (old money) but it was the habit of the poor families to buy half a loaf, the top half would cost 1$^1/_2$d and the bigger bottom half 2d. One may wonder why buy half a loaf when more would be needed within a short time, there by hangs a complicated tale.

In the first place, we hadn't got the money to pay for even half a loaf. This wasn't like the posh people who pay once a month, this was poverty at its lowest level. This is where the 'strap book' comes in, (why it was called 'strap' book is beyond me!). When you could not pay for groceries, you took the 'strap book' with you and the shop-keeper would write in the amount owed which was to be paid off at the weekend. I suppose this was a form of 'interest free' credit. But my mother owed money to three or four of these dingy litle 'strap' shops. She would pay a bit off here, a bit off there, get refused here, get refused there. That was where the apples and oranges came from at Christmas – if you were lucky. The deep rooted 'strap' went on in my family for years, and how my mother fed and clothed ten children in those grim times I will never know, especially when some shops were saying enough's enough.

There was one little treat our mother used to give us, now and again. She would send one of us kids to the shop, with a teacup, for two ounces of jam. The shopkeeper would weigh the cup first on the scales, and from a big brown jar he would put the jam in the cup with a wooden spoon. I am not going to say that we never had a jar of jam in the house, but it was very rare. Being so many of us, we would only get a thin scraping of jam each out of the cup, and my mother would give me two

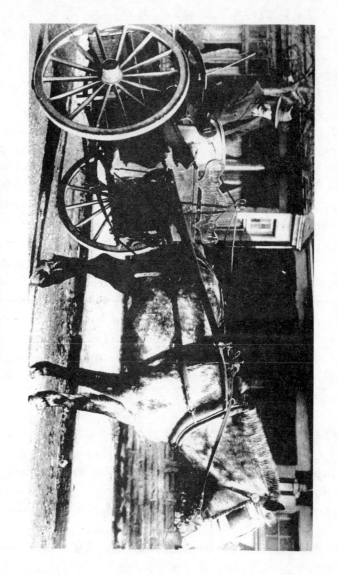

Milk Float in Station Road, Cotteridge, c. 1937

pieces of bread one margarine and one jam, I used to eat the margarine piece of bread first and the jam last, just to kid myself it had all been jam.

There was one good thing in those days. It was a lot cheaper to do a good old stew than fancy food, even though it would be scrag ends of mutton bones. My mother used to put dumplings in the stew as big as cricket balls and just as heavy, these would fill us up even though they were only made with flour and water. There was another cheap meal my mother used to do, that was to buy half a pigs head for a shilling, she would boil it in a big black cast iron pot, till the meat fell off. There were the tripe shops, that sold hot tripe, chitterlings, pigs feet, chawl, faggots and peas, all with gravy. There would be a long queue at the tripe shop on a Friday night, all would be customers with jugs and bowls of every description.

Sometimes my mother would manage to buy a piece of meat for the Sunday dinner, this would be hung on a long chain in front of the fire to cook, with a dish underneath to catch the fat. When we were kids, we had to take it in turns to sit by the meat and turn it in case it burnt, we had to baste the meat with a spoon from the dish below. There were bags, full of stale cakes to be had then, at less than half the price. There was also rotten or badly bruised apples, oranges, and tomatoes, at a penny a bag. The poor people used to gather outside the butchers' shops late on Saturday nights, just before they closed for then they would auction the meat off cheap, even though some of the butchers were open on Sunday mornings.

This garage was in Aston Road – a short distance from Aston Cross.
Petrol, in those days, was 1/3d per gallon (8p)!
The man and the old bicycles were well-known for many years.

Some of the poor kids, myself included used to stand outside the factories to beg for left over sandwiches from the workmen coming out, there were no works canteens then. I can still hear myself saying in proper back street lingo "Gorreny lunch mate"? There was no need for this really, I did have my bread and lard, poor as we were, I can't say I relished those oily thumb marked sandwiches. There were soup kitchens then for the unemployed, where a man out of work could get a bowl of soup, a piece of bread and a cup of tea – free. One was at Thorp Street Barracks and my father went there a few times, I don't think he relished it.

Milk was still being sold from milk churns around the streets, although milk bottles were taking over. Coal was 1/6d per cwt (8p today), and it was my job everyday, (after going to the shop for bread and lard), to fetch a 14lb. bucket of coal from the coalyard. We couldn't afford even $^1/_2$ cwt. of coal, unless it was for the weekend.

Here is how a young working teenager would spend the biggest part of his Saturday pocket money, bearing in mind that his weekly wage would be about 50p, in today's money.

Haircut 3d
Cinema 3d
Ice-cream 1d
Chocolate 1d
Tram there and
back if need be ... 2d
Fish & chips 2d
Total 1/-
(5p in today's money)

It may be interesting for the younger readers to add up the cost of the above in todays prices.

When I left school at fourteen and started to work, the very first thing I bought out of my 2 shillings (10p) pocket money was: 1 egg, 2 ounzes of bacon, ¹/₂ a loaf of bread, 1 bottle of milk – a total of 6¹/₂d or less than 3p in today's money. I cooked these to make a meal while on my own in the house. My mother having dashed out shopping with the rest of my 10/- (50p) weekly wage! I shall never forget that meal, for I have never tasted or enjoyed anything like it before or since.

Then you could buy a shirt and 2 loose collars for 10p in today's money. I bought a pair of new suede shoes for 2/6d (12¹/₂p) even though they fell to pieces on the Lickey Hills a few weeks later. Looking back, things seemed cheap then, but when a working man's wage was £2 to £3 per week, things weren't so cheap. This showed itself in the number of ragged children about in those days. It was nothing to see a young lad with no socks on and with not one toe but with all his toes sticking out of a bursted pair of old boots. You don't see many kids today going around with a dirty filthy shirt tail hanging out of the rear of a much patched pair of trousers. Even those could have been a pair of his older brother's trousers cut off at the knee. Boy's did not wear long trousers like they do today, and it was not uncommon for a lad to start work, still wearing his short knee length trousers which he had worn to school. A boy or girl of working age of fourteen, was only half the size of the kids of today.

November 1930
One of my sisters is ill with diphtheria.

Reflections

My sister had caught diphtheria, and was taken away by ambulance. Under the circumstances and it being a fever, the back street people were still calling these kind of ambulances, 'The Fever Vans', and indeed mothers told their children to keep away from our house, for a few days at least. My mother and father were told that the health department men would come to the house at eight o'clock next morning to fumigate all the rooms. Two men came early next morning, and they put lighted sulphur candles in all the rooms and on the staircase. They then told my mother and father that they would have to lock up and vacate the house until five o'clock that evening. My mother went to my grandmother's, with a couple of the younger kids, I galloped the streets all day, with an occasional dash round to my grandmother's for a dollop of bread and marg., and I think the old man spent most of the day in the public library.

I think it would be fitting here to say a few words about the house and terrace or yard we lived in. Our house had the bare necessities with bare boards in the attic and bedroom, and a bare quarry floor in the living room, The rent was 4/6d per week (22^{1}/$_{2}$p). The living room was lit with a paraffin oil lamp, and the other rooms with candles. Everything was cooked on the fire. (This was not some remote village, this was a street in the centre of the second biggest city in the country). At meal times — it all depended on what was going — newspaper would be spread on the rough scrubbed table top to act as the tablecloth. There were 32 people living off the yard

This photograph of a typical 'Rag & Bone Shop' in Bloomsbury Street, Nechells, (now Nechells Parkway) was taken at the turn of the century, but this place was still there in the 1920s where you could buy a pair of old boots for 4d – in most cases – fit only for the dustbin. Rabbit skins were sold there for many more years.

38

at that time, sharing four toilets and one water tap. All the toilets were kept locked and if there was someone in your toilet and you were in a painful hurry, that was your bad luck. I can honestly say that in over thirty years I was connected with the street, and up to the time of demolition, I never saw a brush of paint put on any of the houses, and I would say, that the houses had not been painted from when they were built in 1896 to being demolished as part of slum clearance in 1957. The only painted houses, were the public houses – the bright lights would draw the men and women to spend the housekeeping money, like gullible moths. There was a system called the 'slate' where a man could have his beer and pay for it at the weekend, that was a little before my time. Many of the backyard terraces were just stinking hovels, where even the cleanest child could catch impetigo or diphtheria.

January 1931

My mother gave me 4d today (less than 2p) to buy a pair of old boots from the rag & bone shop.

Reflections

When the boots I had on, had reached the flip flop stage, whereby I was walking on my bare toes, my mother would give me about 4d to buy an old pair from old Mr. Hunt of the rag & bone shop. He must have been getting on towards 90 years of age then (1925-30) and he would have been a young lad, when Charles Dickens was writing his novels! As I said before he could have been one of the characters stepping straight out from one of Dickens' books. I can see him now, he had grey unkempt hair, his dirty face was wrinkled and pock-marked, with a large bulbous nose, his eyes were just narrow slits. He used to walk from the back of the shop with an aged

39

A house converted into small factories (which made Birmingham famous as the city of a thousand trades). Aston Road, 1934. Note: the small wooden truck to the bottom left – the main means of transporting goods.

hunched shuffle, and his old black coat was going green with age. His dark dingy shop, stunk with old clothes that were stacked on the counter and all around, almost up to the ceiling, and they had been there for years. The shop was lit by an old oil lamp hanging in the window, where he kept his old boots and shoes and other bric-a-brac. On a Monday, after he had been on his rag & bone round, his shop would be full of shoving and pushing women going over the fresh supply of old clothes, just like any shop today at the start of the sales. He wasn't a bad old stick, even though some of us kids used to play him up at times. He only spoke with a whisper at the best of times, and his mouth would open and shut with nothing coming out, and I am sure he would have liked to have got me by the scruff of the neck – dear old Mr. Hunt. There were many women and girls running round in those days with a pair of second-hand drawers from Mr. Hunt's. If he couldn't fix me up with a pair of boots there were plenty of rag & bone shops about.

Now and again, my mother would give me 9d or 10d (about 4p) and tell me to go to Gosta Green Market. Now for those who did not know Gosta Green let me explain. The Rag Market was in a square facing what is now Aston University. The old boots there would be cleaned and polished with some repairs. For me, child-like, it would be like going to Rackhams nowadays.

I have never been able to understand why the word bone in rag & bone shop, it must have come from the days when they collected bones for the handles of knives or for buttons.

Another character who could have stepped right out of Dickens was old Mrs. Dyers who looked about the same age as

These were the days before washing machines – showing the heavy cast iron mangle or clothes wringer. The lady on the right is holding what was called a 'dolly'. This was a large round wooden block with a long wooden handle – the whole thing being rather heavy. The clothes in the wooden tub were pounded with the dolly to remove the dirt – this method went back many years.

Although, in this picture, the lady is smiling it must be remembered that in the '20s a lot of women worked long hours in a cold wash-house washing other people's dirty washing for a few coppers (old pennies). This was especially true with an unemployed husband and a house full of kids.

old man Hunt, about 90. She used to wear a long black frock with long sleeves and a high neck – a proper old Victorian woman. She owned a dark, dingy, sweet shop, lit by an oil lamp, and she also sold bread pudding which was a 1d a lump. After a dollop of that you wouldn't want to go swimming for a couple of hours!

There was also a dingy butcher's shop down the street, and I think the big red faced butcher thought more of his beer than he did his meat! He had a big round purple nose which must have cost a fortune in beer and whisky to get it like that. I used to run a few errands for him, and I don't think he had cold storage or anywhere to keep the meat. One hot summer's morning he gave me a great big bucket of meat, that must have been lying there all the weekend, to take home. I could hardly lift the bucket and the big red nosed butcher said "When you get it home, pour some strong salt water over it". In between dragging the meat home and driving the dogs away, I was really proud to think that there would be enough meat to last all the family for a week. To cut a long story short, the meat stunk the house out. I don't think the maggots had quite shown themselves, but my mother, poor as we were, threw it in the dustbin. I don't know what the dustmen thought a few days later. Needless to say the butcher, and his big red nose, closed down some time later.

June 1931

Had to go into hospital today, (this episode was to play a major part in my life for many years to come).

Reflections

For many weeks I had an ulcerated eye and eventually I had to go into the Eye Hospital for about three weeks, mainly through neglect. I had never been in hospital before and those three weeks I shall never forget.

There wasn't any room in the children's ward and I was put into the men's ward where I was the only young lad. I must have looked a thin, pale, little scruff, because the men patients completely spoiled me. (I think the hospital kept me in longer than need be), I never had so much chocolate, oranges, apples, grapes, bananas, lemonade, and food in all my life. Can you imagine it, a whole egg for breakfast, with as much thin cut bread and butter as you wanted, and cooked dinners, and tea, jam, and cake, cocoa and bread and dripping. Four meals a day, everyday, and proper bed clothes, and real (hospital) pyjamas and my own white towel.

The impact of all this, may be better understood, when all I had been used to was bread and lard, bug infested beds, buckets of urine, and begging left-over sandwiches outside factory gates. I am not going to bore any reader with all the details, but when my father fetched me out of the hospital, it was pouring with rain and my mother was drying a pile of washing around the fire. I am not ashamed to say it, and even though I was nearly twelve, within half an hour of coming home from the hospital, I was on the attic bed sobbing my heart out. Coming home to the grim reality was too much, and my mother never, ever, knew about that little bit of drama and tragedy in the attic.

March 1932
I had to take a bundle of washing to the pawnshop.

Reflections
   Most times my mother would take bundles of washing to the pawnshop, but if she knew there would be a queue, she used to

send one of us kids round, and we would say to the woman "Mom will be round later to pick up the money". My mother, (needless to say), was well known at the pawnshop, and the kindly woman pawnbroker would help in many ways in robbing 'Peter to pay Paul' – this is too complicated to explain here.

My mother had a special little bundle which she kept in the pawnshop for which she would renew the pawn ticket for a few coppers (old pence) now and again, (part of the complications). In this bundle was a white tablecloth, my mother's one and only decent dress and other bits and pieces. She would get this little bundle out of the pawnshop on special occasions, especially when my aunt came up from London.

One day I took a bundle of washing to the pawnshop that my mother had put together in a hurry. The woman there said "Tell your mother I can't take these, they are still wet".

My mother was in two or three little clothes clubs, to which she would pay so much each week. She would perhaps buy two of my sisters a dress each. Within a few days the dresses would vanish. I leave you to guess where they had gone! There was also a moneylender who used to call for his weekly payment.

It may be thought that my mother was a poor manager, but when you have little or no money coming in, and you've got a houseful of hungry children to feed, day in and day out, every means has to be used.

If you are a woman, can you imagine bearing 10 children and having to wash other people's clothes in an outside wash-house, lit by a candle during a dark winter's day. Think about it – it really was part of my mother's lot for many years.

It is obvious that my mother must have half-starved herself to feed us kids, and it is a fact that I have seen my mother leave the wash-house for a few minutes to feed the tenth baby. She looked faint with the baby at her breast. It seemed that washing clothes and the 10th baby at her breast was just too much.

Apart from the pawnshop next door to where we lived, there were many others in the Nechells area of Birmingham. At each one there were daily queues both inside and out, especially on a Monday morning. From the middle of the 1930s, people were being moved out from the city to new estates on the outskirts but they still travelled back to Nechells and the pawnshops. These pawnshop journeys carried on well into the late 1950s when that area of Nechells with its pawnshops was demolished. It is said that the buses and trams carrying these people and their pawnshop bundles were know as *THE PAWNSHOP SPECIALS!!*

This may be the right time to say a few words in defence of my father, although perhaps he doesn't deserve it. He was born in 1879. His mother died early and his father was killed by a traction engine at a fairground when both my father and his brother were young children. They were brought up by some woman who took them in, even though she had kids of her own and up to her neck in poverty. My father had run the streets in his bare feet, and was bashed from pillar to post, all his life, so I suppose there is some understanding for his irresponsible ways. Perhaps it is worth pointing out that he was unemployed not by choice, but was a victim of the depression years of the 20s and 30s when some 3 million were unemployed.

Going from the sublime to the ridiculous, there was the time, when one of my sisters met my father in the street and said, "Hello Dad", my father replied "Which one are you?".

November 1932
My father has to go on the Parish.

Reflections
Being unemployed in the 1920s was a lot more soul destroying and tragic than it is today. One of the gross injustices of the 'Means Test' was having to sell some of the contents of your home before you were given any money, even to buy food. Even then you were only given the bare minimum on which to survive. For example, my father was instructed, by the Means Test inspector, to sell an old sewing machine which we had. This fetched 4/6d and even that was deducted from his allowance.

There was a step down even from the 'Means Test' into what was known as 'The Parish'. Here no money was given to the poor and only a bare minimum of food and coal was given on the showing of a card. No allowance was made for clothing and lighting.

I don't know how The Parish affected other people, but in my father's case, when he was on the Means Test, he was seen going into a pub by an inspector. His money was then stopped and he was put on The Parish, to protect us children and our mother.

Let me pause for a moment to mention one or two bits and pieces, which were part of our lives in the 1920s and early 1930s.

Going on holiday to the seaside was a rare thing for back street people in those times. In fact, I never saw the sea until I was in my teens. There was no such thing as holidays with pay. For those in work the main holiday was three days off without pay.

You don't hear the "Bulls" (sirens) today. They used to give out the time of day.

It was an offence to shake mats in the street after nine o'clock in the morning. You could be fined 10/- for a chimney fire.

If you were receiving State sickness benefit of 7/6d, you had to be in the house by nine o'clock at night, or rather that was the rule. A doctor would charge 4/6 if he was called out. An ambulance could cost as much as 7/6 if you were working or had a doctor's note.

You don't see gangs of kids with barrows fetching loads of coal and coke for pocket money, which everyone used to do in those days. There were yards with hundreds of old, battered bicycles for the kids, to hire at 2d an hour. The kids would buy a 1d swede or a pomegranate or a stick of spanish juice, to eat in the pictures (cinema) they would last a long time.

September 1933
Came home from school today, and found my mother ill in bed.

Reflections.

When I came home my mother, who was ill in bed, looked terrible. With a weak voice she told me to fetch one of the neighbours. The neighbour had only been there a few minutes, when my mother vomited mouthfulls of blood. It was all over the bed and the neighbour (a little ragged woman) said, "Oh God don't let her die". My mother was rushed to hospital and for many weeks she was in a bad way. It turned out that a stomach ulcer or ulcers had burst. She must have been in agony for weeks or even months. It seemed that the strain of the years with 10 kids, the washing, pawning, scrubbing, together with having starved herself to feed us, had at last taken its toll. The following weeks were chaos for there was other people's wet washing in the brewhouse, washing that she had actually been doing when she was taken ill. There was other people's washing in the pawnshop; there were piles of washing waiting to be ironed; there were the younger kids to be bathed and fed and 'Tom, Dick, and Harry', to be paid for food we already had on the strap. As ill as she was within a couple of days, she told my sisters to bring an old purse, (in which she kept her pawn tickets), to the hospital. She wanted to sort them out and tell my sisters, which washing to get out of the pawnshop using my father's unemployment pay. Can the reader for a moment, imagine my mother, lying ill with her hands shaking, trying to sort out pawn tickets on the hospital bed yet this is all quite true. Is it any wonder, as was mentioned in the introduction, that for what she had gone through, she deserved a medal equivalent to the Victoria Cross.

My two older, and now married sisters, did all they could, (both financially and otherwise), while my mother was in hospital, but they were as poor as church mice themselves, and

49

I think most of the kind neighbours, got their own washing out that she had pawned. Most of the bundles of washing pawned, were only for a couple of bob, but that would buy us all our food for a day or more. For three or four weeks after my mother came out of hospital, my sisters and neighbours continued to give us all the help they could, but they were all poor, and in the same boat themselves. After the months of agony leading up to the blood soaked bed, and the little neighbour praying for her life, within a couple of weeks of leaving hospital, my mother was back in the wash-house and pawnshop.

Final Reflections.

Looking back, I have wished many times that I had been more help to my mother's unhappy lot. But a housefull of kids, pawnshop, bread and lard and two ounces of jam in a tea cup, was a way of life then, and we kids just didn't realise the tragedy of it all over 60 years ago. I came across an old photograph taken of my mother when she was about 44 years of age, she is not wearing her wedding ring. It was a known fact in the family that she had pawned it some years before never to be seen again. She had bought a threepenny or sixpenny brass ring from Woolworths in place of the original. Through the years of extreme poverty and bringing up the family, she had a saying intended for the ears of my father, and any of my sisters getting married, "Buy your own wedding ring, buy your own strife!" I don't know why she is not wearing even her brass "wedding ring" in the photograph.

One Last Look!

Our old house, the pawnshop and the pub where my father spent a life-time were demolished in the slum clearances of the 1950s.

In their place was built a new church! In a silly sort of way I would like to think that the church was built in memory of my mother for her years of sacrifice. I am sure that somewhere in the foundations of that church there must be a scattering of my mother's discarded pawn tickets.

It is a funny thing, my mother met and married my father when she worked in a little cook shop in a side street in the city centre of Birmingham. That was before buying her own wedding ring, the ten kids and the burst ulcers.

The name of that street?
NEEDLESS ALLEY
What mockery!

R.I.P.

This book was originally written in 1983 and is now finally being printed and published. With reflection even now in 1989, when one is a little older and maybe wiser, there is nothing to alter in the original script.

SOME ADVICE AND POETRY

**Free to sit and free to think,
Free to pay for what you drink;
Free to stop an hour or so,
When uneasy, free to go.**

In GOD we trust: all others CASH.

My beer is good, my measure just,
Forgive me please, I cannot trust;
I have trusted many to my sorrow –
So pay today and owe tomorrow.

My clocks tick, but I don't.

2 pints make .... 1 quart
4 quarts make .... 1 gallon
1 argument makes .... 1 quarrel
1 quarrel makes .... 1 fight
1 fight makes .... 2 policemen
1 magistrate .... 20/- or 14 days

When you swear, swear by your country.

When you steal, steal away from bad company.

When you drink, drink with EVERETT at the EAGLE.

**Call frequently,
Drink moderately,
Pay honourably,
Be good company,
Part friendly,
Go home quietly.**

I have been pleasing and displeasing the public ever since I started.

I have also been cussed and discussed, robbed, lied to, held up, hung up and knocked up. The only reason I am staying in business is to see what the hell will happen next.
Life is just one dammed thing after another.

A notice in a public house – early 1930

Ye Olde Swan, Washwood Heath.

53

One or two steam wagons were still being used round the streets in the 1920s.

Two letters to the *Birmingham Mail* **published in 1930**

Sir, I noticed a photograph in the 'Mail' of a policeman on point duty in Wolverhampton with a kind of sunshade over him, stating it was too hot for him. I thought it very amusing to see such a thing.

I am sure in time they will have motor cars to ride about in and all out of the ratepayers' money.

The idea of paying a policeman about £3 5s. or £3 10s., when I have to work in front of a furnace for £2 5s. and nothing to shelter me from the heat! Is a policeman worth £3 5s. or £3 10s and a uniform, being an unskilled man? No wonder the rates are so high.

I consider £2 10s. quite enough for unskilled labour, and they get all consideration.

2 Hot

Reader's letter, August 8, 1930

SERVANTS

Sir, Until maids are treated as human beings instead of machines, the problem is still to be solved.

As for 'idleness', I could laugh when I think of some of the jobs I have had. Sixteen hours a day with no off-duty, one half-day per week, when you feel like crawling into bed instead of going out.

Even when trying to eat a meal some paltry thing will get you up, if only to let the overfed mongrel out and again to be let in.

No doubt there are some good, kind mistresses but their maids' jobs are never to let.

Had Some

August 7, 1930

Reproduced by kind permission of the 'Birmingham Post & Mail'

The 'Bull Ring' in Birmingham, early 1930s.

Albert Ketèlby

Two pieces of music are mentioned by the author in this book *In A Monastery Garden* and *In A Persian Market*. Unknown to the author was the fact that the composer of these two favourites of that period – Albert W. Ketèlby was born in Birmingham on August 4th 1875 and it is believed that his real name was William Aston. He showed early musical promise and studied in Birmingham under A.R. Gaul and Dr. Herbert Wareing. At the age of eleven he composed a piano sonata which was performed at Worcester and won the praise of Sir Edward Elgar. At thirteen he won the Queen Victoria Scholarship to Trinity College, London, where he studied piano under G.E. Bambridge, harmony and composition under Dr. Gordon Saunders, also various instruments including the cello, clarinet, French horn, oboe and organ. Although the cello remained his favourite instrument but he was also accomplished organist.

Perhaps it was his ability on the various musical instruments which made his composition such favourites of the 1920s and 1930s. Even today many people will recognise the tunes within his music but not necessarily the actual titles.

As a matter of interest *In A Monastery Garden* was composed in 1915 and *In A Persian Market* in 1920.

An early (1920s) char-a-banc (coach outing).
For most of the back street people, going to Bewdley or Stratford was almost a foreign country, bearing in mind that a lot of the older people had never left the street or district they were born and died in. Going to the seaside was a rare event indeed. Any family lucky enough was waved off by those left behind!

58

A Birmingham Transport electric tram seen here in Pershore Road, Cotteridge.

Horses and carts on Saltley High Street in the 1920s

Further Reflections – Part III

My Father

As was mentioned earlier, my father was a drunken layabout, but poverty, drunken fathers, and a house full of kids, was a way of life in those days. My father was a well-known character around the district, and apart from being a bit of a 'comedian' himself, would do anything for a laugh.

He came in the house one day and said to my mother
People speak to me in the street and I don't know who they are. If I walked past the pyramids in Egypt, I am sure one of the arabs would say: Good Morning Tom .

My mother and all us kids were sitting in the house, one Saturday evening, when at about 10 p.m. the front door flew open and in staggered the old man, stinking drunk, and being dragged on a rope by the biggest billy goat you have ever seen, which was also drunk! Amidst all the screams from all us kids, the cat shot over the table, knocking over the sugar basin – from then on it was chaos. Someone had given the goat to the old man, and all the poor thing had been given to eat and drink in the public houses were handfulls of cigarette ends and pints of beer! So what with being drunk, the goat messed all round the room, dropping round pellets of dung as it dashed round and round the table.

In the midst of all the chaos there was my mother, wringing her hands and shouting
"Get that stinking drunken goat out of here",
and all us kids screaming with delight. To add to this, my two older sisters came in with their boyfriends (and future husbands) having been out for the evening.

No one slept that night, except the drunken old man having by now staggered to bed – I'm sure he would have taken the goat with him! The sisters' boyfriends had dragged the goat down into the cellar and tied it to the wall with a rope. They then went home holding their sides with laughter. The naying of the goat kept us awake all night and my two sisters took it in turns to go down to the goat in the cellar to console it.

The next morning, my father dragged the goat out of the house, or rather the goat dragged him, and he sold the beast for 2/6d (12½p) which was another 5 pints of beer to be drunk.

Another example of my father's comical ways was the time he borrowed a great big Chinese coolie type straw hat that must have measured nearly three feet across the brim. He put the hat on, and then stripped naked to the waist – he was tall and very thin – so you can imagine the sight. He then borrowed one of those schoolboy type air pellet rifles and being a hot summer Bank Holiday went round all the pubs, full of devilment. He told everybody that he had just come back from big game hunting in Africa and, needless to say, he had to be carried back home with his straw hat and rifle, absolutely stinking blotto.

This, then, is a couple of examples of the many comical tricks my father got up to – you can see why he was always drunk on free beer. Perhaps one should mention that both his mother and father had died when he was only a small child leaving him to run the back streets of Victorian England in his bare feet. I sometimes think that beneath his comical make-up there was, in reality, a very broken-hearted man.

The Old Clock at Aston Cross
A well-known Victorian landmark

'Daily Mail' Clothes

As I mentioned page 39, now and again my mother would give me 4d (old pence) to go and buy a pair of boots from the Rag and Bone Shop.

But there was something else that happened every year at the coming of winter. This was the free issue of new boots and clothes from the 'Daily Mail Charity for Poor Children'. I forget how many times I had this free isuue but I don't think the scheme started until the late 1920s.

I can recall one time when my father took me and my sister to this big warehouse somewhere in the back streets for the free issue of 'Daily Mail' boots and clothing. There were hundreds of kids there together with mothers or fathers. Some were given just boots but if you were really poor then you had clothing as well – needless to say that we had the full issue!

I was given a round neck navy-type black pullover, a pair of knee length brown corduroy school trousers, a pair of heavy black boots and black socks. I am sure my great big heavy boots were made from blocks of cast iron for you could hardly walk in them. It took weeks of pain before the boots would even bend, and if anyone shoved you over, the boots would remain rooted to the ground like two blocks of lead. The girls were given black shoes, black gym slips, etc. etc. When we had our clothes from the warehouse I wanted to keep my old clothes on in case I met any of my school mates but father insisted that we put the workhouse-type clothes on at the warehouse. He herded me and my sister back home like a couple of shuffling zombies. I am sure my corduroy trousers were made of wood.

The reason why I hated the free 'Daily Mail' clothes was that if you wore the full issue, all the kids would shout after you 'Daily Mail', 'Daily Mail', and this would go on for days, to and from school, and after. The sides of the boots and shoes were punched with small pinholes forming the letters D.M. ('Daily Mail'). This was to stop your mother pawning them and the pawnbroker would also be breaking the law by taking them in.

There was only one thing in favour of those boots and that was when they did start to bend, they made smashing football boots!

Note the many studs in the bottom of the boots.
The intention was good, but painfully cruel for all that.

Starting Work

The Diary and Reflections in this book are based on my school years between the ages of 8 and 14. But once again to meet the wishes of readers of the first edition of this book, here are some reflections on my first eighteen months at work after leaving school at 14.

After galloping the back streets since I could walk, I shall never forget the big iron factory gates clanging behind me when I started my first factory job. It was like locking-up a wild animal in a cage – a month was enough then I packed it in. From then on for the next eighteen months, I must have had at least 15 to 20 jobs, of which I will give two humorous examples.

The first, and an example of my couldn't-care-less attitude, was when I got a job at a factory just 2 minutes round the corner from where I lived. I started at 8 a.m. and the foreman took me into a long broken down old workshop with a tin corrugated roof. I was put to work with a fast moving grinding wheel held by hand and had to grind off the rough edges of small castors which were to be fixed to the legs of furniture. It had been snowing overnight and the tin roof had a number of small holes in it. Little did I know that one of these was right over my head! Within minutes the first drop of melted snow dropped on to the back of my neck like an electric shock, to add to my, by now, freezing fingers. I put down the castor I was working on, walked through the workshop, out into the street, and at 8.15 a.m., just fifteen minutes after starting work, was back in the house sitting by the fire with my mother standing there with her hands on her hips and her mouth open!

The second example was when I got a job through a newspaper advertisement for a young lad to assist the travelling Representative at a well-known sauce and pickle factory, now closed down.

I had to be there for 9 a.m. to meet the representative with his pinstripe suit, bowler hat and umbrella, in the office. He then took me outside into the street where someone had parked in front of the office, the most beatuiful covered-in handcart I had ever seen. It had been painted and varnished in a rich dark green with yellow lines on the wheels, body and shafts. The sauce and pickle samples were on shelves behing the sliding doors of the main body of the cart.

I quickly saw that there were two snags. Firstly the gigantic size of the whole outfit, even the shafts were never made for the human frame but for the biggest donkey you could find. Secondly, the area of the first calls was where I lived! If any of my mates saw me shoving that monster, I would never live it down.

The plan was that I had to shove the cart round on a daily routine of shopping areas where the representaive would go into the shops with samples to gain orders. At the very first shop the rep. went into I ran. I ran like mad, never so quick in all my life, jumping over prams and everything else in sight. Within five minutes I was not only home but up in the attic looking through the window, shaking like a leaf. I was there for 2 hours. The time of starting the job to refuge in the attic was ¾ of an hour!

I was expecting the rep. to come down the street, red in the face, shoving the sauce cart, but I don't think he knew where I lived. Anyhow, I expected him to come dashing up the attic stairs any minute to bash me with his umbrella. I wonder for how many years and times the rep. told his friends and relations the tale of the missing assistant and the abandoned sauce cart.

Also, I wonder if the foreman at the castor making factory ever told the tale of the young lad who worked in his factory for less than 15 minutes and just vanished.

Some readers may not see any humour in my early wayward ways, but within a few weeks, I went into the adventurous and travelling building trade. I was a bricklayer for 35 years and despite 35 painful winters spent outside, it seemed I had found my calling.

Old Mrs. Dyer's Shop

I mentioned earlier, old Mrs. Dyer who kept a dingy little sweet shop, with the oil lamp in the window and from whom I bought many a dollop of her delicious Bread Pudding.

That was until a couple of school-mates (who lived near the old lady's shop) told me that when it was dark at night, and the shop was shut, they had stood by the shop window, and by the light of the street lamp had watched dozens of mice galloping amongst the sweets in the shop window. Bearing in mind that like other kids, I had bought many a lump of the old lady's bread pudding, and thinking of the mice I have often wondered if the black currants on the top of the bread pudding were really currants!

Because of the mice droppings, I didn't go to old Mrs. Dyer's dingy old shop again, which was a pity really, as I can still taste those wonderful chunks of delicious currant filled bread puddings – mice droppings or not!

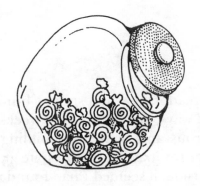

'The Boys Brigade'

The reader must by now have realised that I was a ragged little scruff, like so many young kids in those days. But it was a sign of the times and the poor back street kids took ragged clothes for granted.

Further proof of my ragged state was the time I joined the Boys Brigade at a local church. We had a parade one Sunday morning, when all the Brigade were lined up outside the church hall and then marched round the back streets, led by a band of 2 buglers and 2 drummers, to show the people the good work the Boys Brigade was doing.

About half-an-hour before the parade was to assemble, I called on my young friend who was in the Brigade and who lived facing the church hall. I think he was an orphan because he lived with his two old maiden aunts, but he was always well-dressed and well looked after.

This is where my ragged clothes come into it, because when my friend's aunts saw my ragged knee length trousers with my shirt tail hanging out of a hole in my backside, they were shocked and disgusted. They did no more but sorted out a pair of my friend's trousers, and told me to go into a backroom and change into them. My friend was a lot bigger and taller than me in every way, and the posh trousers went round me twice over, but after much pulling and tucking, the two aunts convinced me that they didn't look too bad.

I wish I had a photograph of me in those large baggy trousers flapping in the wind well below my knees, as I marched in time with the band around the back streets over 60 years ago. The trousers were only held up with a belt and being two or three sizes too big, and having to swing my arms when marching, I was expecting the trousers to drop around my ankles at anytime. You must remember that in those days underpants were unknown to me and it would not have been a pretty sight if I had needed to bend down to pull them back up.

I joined the Boys Brigade when I was 9 years of age. The Captain in charge was a kind man about 50 years old. His devotion to the Brigade was such that it is only with kindness that I mention that it was with some humour amongst us boys that the Captain had a nervous twitch in one eye.

In fact it was more than a twitch, it was a complete eye closing wink over which he had no control. I did not know about the Captain's eye-winking twitch, and when I first met him he said,
"So you are the new boy",
and gave one of his winks. I just stood there not knowing whether I had got to wink back or not.

When we had our drill training sessions in the church hall, the Captain would line us up – army style – and then shout "Attention" and then wink his eye. We would all spring smartly to attention and it was hard for us not to fall over from laughing because of the Captain's winks.

Having said all that, and to prove how good and caring the Captain was, I must mention what happened when I missed one of the meetings. The next evening the Captain called at my home, to ask why I had not attended the usual meeting. He was concerend that I was not ill or anything and wanted to know if he could be of help – that was the kind of person he was.

It was common to have 8,10 or 12 children in one family.
Here's just a few – living in one backyard – late 1920s.

A typical back yard of the late 1920s
This is only the corner of a square of broken down, bug infested houses.

Forgotten Workmen

Years ago, labourers employed digging holes or trenches, had to buy their own shovels, and if they had not got their own shovel, they would not get a job.

Therefore, having his own shovel was of great value to the labourer (or navvy as he was called) and he would clean and polish his shovel until it shone like silver. The shovels were so clean and polished, they would be used as 'frying pans' for the labourers mid-morning breakfast or lunchtime fry-up. wherever they were working.

In about 1928, a lot of major work was going on in our street. Not only installing gas to all the houses, but also laying water pipes and water taps to all the houses as well.

The workmen would start work at 7.30 a.m. and so before 9.00 a.m. they would be sitting down to breakfast, in the street, around a fire bucket cooking bacon and eggs on their shovels. So you can imagine me on my way to school, with a slice of cold toast wrapped in a newspaper for my mid-morning break at school, standing and looking at a group of these workmen sitting round the fire cooking their breakfast on the shovels.

On a cold morning, the warmth from the workmen's fire, the smell of frying eggs and bacon, and steaming hot tea, would make many half-starved kids like me think to themselves "If I had a lot of money, I would buy me a shovel and some bacon and eggs".

I have mentioned earlier that the first thing I bought out of my 2/- (10p) pocket money, when I started work at 14, was 1 egg, 2 ounces of bacon, half a loaf of bread and a bottle of milk which cost 6½d (less than 3p nowadays). It seems that even 60 years later, the memory of sizzling eggs and bacon on the shovels is still with me.

It has been said that, in those days, if there was no work about and a labourer could not get a job, he would pawn his shovel at the nearby pawnbrokers for the price of a couple of pints of beer.

Delivery Van in Bournville Village around 1912

More 'Characters'

I have written about some of the characters of the 1920s and 30s in other parts of the book, but others keep coming to mind.

There was the ragged character, and also his ragged wife, who were always together as they went round the streets every day gathering old rags, scrap metal or any old junk in an old box-shaped barrow on two wheels. At the end of the day, they would sell the old junk to the nearest rag & bone yard for a couple of bob and then go to the nearest public house to spend the profits – 2/- (10p) in those days would buy 6 pints of beer.

You could always tell when our ragged friend and his wife had had a good day because towards evening would find them on their way home. Him lying in the bottom of the box-barrow – stinking drunk, with his legs stuck up in the air – she, his wife, would be staggering left and right pushing him and the barrow. She having had her fill, it was only the barrow that was holding her up. Happy Days!

There was 'Barber Brown', who kept a barber's shop at the end of our street, and was a character in many ways. You could always tell when business was slack because you would hear him playing his banjo inside his shop.

I came past his shop, one day, and not only was

Barber Brown playing his banjo, but he and a couple of his old friends and customers were singing all the songs of the day.

It seems that even in the 1920s there was still a touch of the old Victorian and Edwardian eras, of the singing barbers – Happy Days!

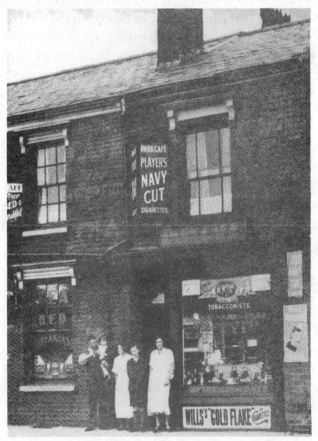

Park Café, Lichfield Road, Aston around 1935

Horses

In the 1920s, there were many horses and carts delivering goods of every description around the streets of Birmingham, as can be seen in many of the photographs in this book.

There were hundreds of railway delivery horses and carts up and down the streets. The daily delivery of milk, bread and coal to the houses was also by horse and cart. In addition there were many hawkers selling their goods from horses and carts.

So can the younger readers imagine all these horses leaving a continual trail of manure on both sides of the streets and roads, because that is how it was in those days. Just think what would be said of those conditions these days!

A brewer's dray in Aston

A fire engine of the Handsworth Brigade at the turn of the century.

Motorcycles on The Green, Kings Norton at about 1922

A steam tram in Birchfield Road, Perry Bar.
All those wires and posts came later!

81

Clay Pipes and Tobacco

Years ago, many men smoked clay pipes. These were so cheap that when the pipes broke they were just thrown away. Because so many men smoked pipes in public houses, these had 'spitoons' (a dish to spit in!) on different parts of the bar floor. The floors were also covered with sawdust for those whose aim was not too good. Now you know why bars traditionally had sawdust on the floor!.

My father used to send me to the shop for a 'penny-weight' of twist. This was a stick or hard lump of black tobacco. The shopkeeper would put a penny on one side of the scales and weigh out the tobacco on the other, so it was a penny's weight not a penny's worth.

For all the poverty and rags of the bad old days, when I reflect on all the oddities and the many characters of those times, I still find myself saying – Happy Days.

Epilogue: DO YOU REMEMBER?

Do you remember
The horses, the pawnshops, the street?
Do you remember
When barrel organs, were a treat?

Do you remember
The games we played,
Tip cat, and kick the can,
On hot Summer's days?

Do you remember
The singers in the gutter.
When bread and lard
Was back street butter?

Do you remember
The old cart horses
With May Day ribbons,
And blacksmith's forges?

Do you remember
Trotters, and faggots and peas,
And ragged kids
With dirty knees?

Do you remember
The pawnshop queues.
The bedsheets taken
To pay the dues?

Do you remember
The rag and bone shop.
Fourpence for old boots
When yours dropped off?

Do you remember
"IN A MONASTERY GARDEN"
The knockers up, and four shilling rent.
You do?- then, Happy Retirement!

J.F.   1983

Family Tree

Date of Birth	The Family	Age in 1926	Why left home	Age when died
1879	Father	47	–	74
1886	Mother	40	–	73
1906	Girl	20	Married 1928	31
1908	Girl	18	Married 1930	76
1910	Boy	16	New Zealand	Lost contact
1912	Girl	14	Domestic 1926	34
ALL THE CHILDREN ABOVE HAD LEFT HOME BY 1930 These were the best years for my parents, before the poverty days.				
1915	Girl	Age in 1930 15	Married 1934	36
1918	Girl	12	Married 1935	Alive 1989
1920	Boy	10	Called up (Army)	Alive 1989
1922	Boy	8	Called up (Army)	Alive 1989
1924	Girl	6	A.T.S. 1942	Alive 1989
1930	Boy	Baby	Nat. Service	Alive 1989

by Winifred Mary Ruston

Illustrated by Ruth Hadfield

Polly and Alice

As a direct result of the publication of the first edition of this book Volcano was offered another book reflecting social history of a bygone era.

This unusual book is in two parts. The first, a story for children was written some years ago but never published.

It is in reality an autobiography set in villages in Northamptonshire during the 19th century. The second part provides a factual background to the story and is a fascinating picture of village life at a time of change from an agricultural to an industrial society.

The book contains unique archive material by way of drawings and photographs – the earliest being 1816.

To anyone with an interest in British social history and those who may want to introduce children to the subject this book is a must.

First published December 1990

Paperback 148 pages   Price: £3.50

**IN CASE OF DIFFICULTY IN FINDING A COPY
PLEASE SEND YOUR NAME AND ADDRESS
TOGETHER WITH A CHEQUE FOR £3.75 DIRECT TO THE PUBLISHERS**